This handbook belongs to: _____

food smarts

WASTE REDUCTION for KIDS

TABLE OF CONTENTS

LESSON 1: FOOD FLOW FROM FARM TO FORK 3
    WHERE IS THE WASTE 4
    RECIPE - SPICED TRAIL MIX 5

LESSON 2: PLANTING PLANT PARTS 7
    NAME THAT PLANT PART 8
    RECIPE - CUCUMBER DRESSING 9
    RECIPE - PLANT PARTS SALAD 10
    RECIPE - CARROT TOP/HERB DIP 11
    RECIPE - CROSTINI "LITTLE TOASTS" 12

LESSON 3: FOOD SAVING SALSA 13
    MAKE YOUR OWN SALSA 14
    RECIPE - HIP CHIPS 15

LESSON 4: LEFTOVER MAKEOVER 17
    WRITE YOUR OWN RECIPE 18
    WRITE YOUR OWN RECIPE (CONT) 19
    COOKING TERMS 20
    RECIPE - FRENCH TOAST STICKS 21
    RECIPE - ITALIAN BREAD SALAD 22

LESSON 5: DO I THROW IT OUT? 23
    ACTIVITY - PACKAGE SMART 24
    ACTIVITY - GARDEN COMPOSTING 101 25
    RECIPE - HUMMUS AND VEGGIE WRAPS 26
    RECIPE - EASY PEASY FRIED RICE 27

Lesson 1:
Food Flow from Farm to Fork

Lesson 1: Where is the Waste?

According to the USDA, over 30% of the United States' food supply is wasted.

This chart shows you where food is wasted in the US.

Government agencies are now working together to cut US food waste by 50% by 2030.

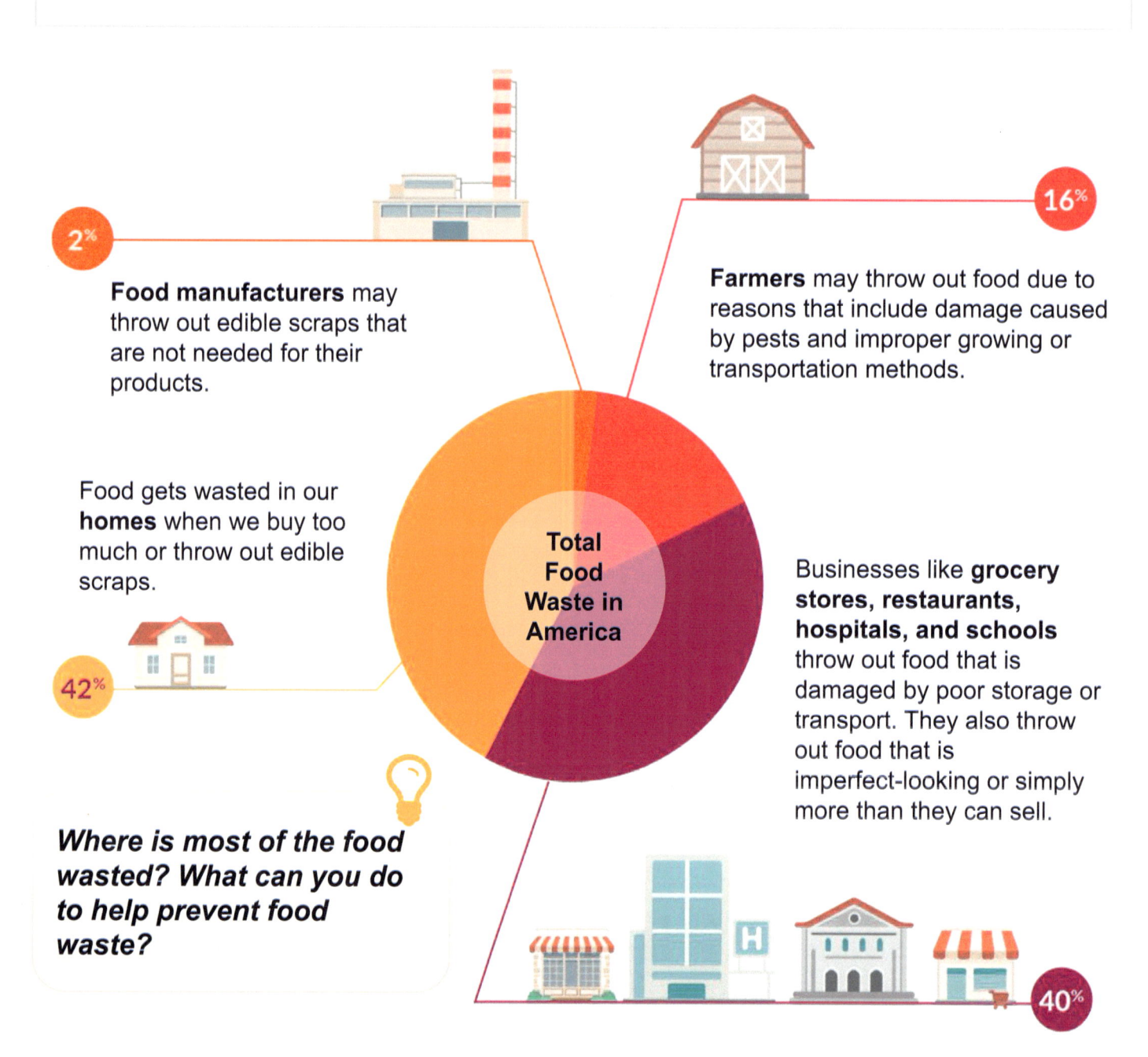

2%

Food manufacturers may throw out edible scraps that are not needed for their products.

16%

Farmers may throw out food due to reasons that include damage caused by pests and improper growing or transportation methods.

Food gets wasted in our **homes** when we buy too much or throw out edible scraps.

42%

Total Food Waste in America

Businesses like **grocery stores, restaurants, hospitals, and schools** throw out food that is damaged by poor storage or transport. They also throw out food that is imperfect-looking or simply more than they can sell.

Where is most of the food wasted? What can you do to help prevent food waste?

40%

Leah's Pantry | *Food Smarts Waste Reduction for Kids* v.05202024

Lesson 1: Recipe

Spiced Trail Mix

🕐 10 minutes

Ingredients

½ cup Nuts

½ cup Dried Fruit

½ cup Sunflower or Pumpkin Seeds

½ cup Pretzels, Toasted Oat or Wheat Squares Cereal, or Mini Crackers

½ cup Shredded Coconut

½ cup Chocolate Chips

Paprika or Cinnamon

Salt to taste

Serves 6

Recipe Directions

1. Toss all ingredients and mix well.
2. Put into small containers or sealed bags to take with you.

Chef's Tips

To bring out the sweet flavor of the ingredients, use cinnamon. For sweet and savory, use paprika and a pinch of salt.

If you have an allergy or are missing an item just leave it out or replace with more of the other ingredients.

Lesson 2:
Planting Plant Parts

Lesson 2: Name that Plant Part

Label the plant parts. What parts of the plant can you eat?

| Fruit | Stem | Leaf |
| Flower | Root | Seed |

Lesson 2: Recipe

1

Cucumber Dressing

🕐 5 minutes

Ingredients

1 cup Plain Greek Yogurt

⅓ cup Olive oil

½ Cucumber, grated

½ Lemon, juiced

1 Green Onion, minced

¼ cup chopped Fresh Herbs– Basil, Parsley, or Cilantro

Salt and Pepper to taste

Serves 4

Recipe Directions

1. Place all ingredients in a screw top jar.
2. Tighten the lid and shake to stir.
3. Pour over Plant Parts Salad (see recipe on next page) or any other green salad and toss.

Chef's Tips

| Try using scissors to mince fresh herbs and green onions. | Save the lemon rind to flavor your water later. | Switch arms when shaking dressing so you don't tire out. |

Leah's Pantry | *Food Smarts Waste Reduction for Kids* v.05202024

Lesson 2: Recipe

Plant Parts Salad

🕐 10 minutes

Ingredients

1 Head Romaine Lettuce, chopped or torn

1 Bunch Green Onions, chopped

2 Carrots, grated

2 Tbsp. Sunflower Seeds

Cucumber Dressing

Serves 4

Recipe Directions

1. Place chopped vegetables and grated carrot in a large bowl.
2. Add dressing and toss.

    Sprinkle with sunflower seeds.

Chef's Tips

Save carrot tops, herbs, and leftover green onions to make the Carrot Top/Herb dip.

Save the bottom 2 inches of the romaine lettuce for planting later.

Save the bottom inch of the green onions with roots for re-growing in soil or jar of water.

Lesson 2: Recipe

Carrot Top/Herb Dip

🕐 10 minutes

Ingredients

¼ cup leftover Carrot Top Greens or fresh herbs
  —well chopped

1 cup softened Cream Cheese

Salt and Pepper

¼ Lemon

Serves 4

Recipe Directions

1. Cut lemon into four pieces and squeeze the juice of one ¼ into bowl with chopped greens, and 1 cup cream cheese.

2. Mix all ingredients together until well blended.

3. Salt and pepper, to taste.

4. Enjoy with crostini, crackers, or cut veggies.

Chef's Tips

Add finely chopped leftover raw veggies for a spring spread.

Use the leftover lemon rind to flavor your water.

Try fresh leafy herbs like dill, basil, parsley, and green onions.

If you use dry or woody herbs, like thyme or rosemary, use less.

Leah's Pantry | *Food Smarts Waste Reduction for Kids v.05202024*

Lesson 2: Recipe

Crostini - "Little Toasts"

🕒 10 minutes

Ingredients

1 Loaf Stale Bread, Bagels, or Pitas.

2 Tbsp. Olive or Vegetable Oil

1 Clove of Garlic, optional

Serves 4

Recipe Directions

1. Preheat oven.
2. Slice bread into thin, small pieces.
3. Rub with peeled garlic clove.
4. Put in a bowl and toss with olive oil.
5. Transfer to baking sheet and cook for 5 minutes at 450 degrees.
6. Enjoy with Carrot Top Dip or Hummus.

Chef's Tips

Sprinkle with parmesan cheese for cheese toast.

Use the heels (ends) of the bread loaf, too.

Use any kind of leftover bread, bagels, or pita.

Store in an airtight container.

Lesson 3:
Food-Saving Salsa

Lesson 3: Make Your Own Salsa

Leah's PANTRY

food smarts — WASTE REDUCTION for KIDS —

← Let's name your recipe

Ingredients

Recipe Directions

Make Your Own Salsa: Choose Your Ingredients

Tomatoes	Chili Powder	Peaches
Onions	Cucumber	Bell Peppers
Lime	Avocado	Corn
Jalapeno	Jicama	_____
Cilantro	Mango	_____
Cumin	Pineapple	_____
Garlic	Watermelon	_____
Black Beans		

Leah's Pantry | *Food Smarts Waste Reduction for Kids* v.05202024

Lesson 3: Recipe

Hip Chips

🕐 10 minutes

Ingredients

4 Tortillas or Pitas, split open

Olive oil

Salt and pepper

Dried herbs: Parsley, Basil

Optional: Taco Seasoning, Ranch Powder, Garlic Powder, Tajin, or Everything Bagel seasoning

Serves 4

Recipe Directions

1. Brush tortillas/pitas with oil on both sides.
2. Add preferred seasonings.
3. Cut into triangles.
4. Spread in one layer on baking sheet.
5. Bake until golden, about 7 minutes at 400 degrees.
6. Enjoy with your favorite dip or salsa.

Chef's Tips

Try whole wheat or corn tortillas.

Chipotle or chili powder gives the chips a kick!

Leftover tortillas, pita, and other flatbread can be toasted then simmered in salsa or spicy tomato sauce for a yummy dish. In Mexico these are called *Chilaquiles*.

Lesson 4:
Leftover Makeover

Lesson 4: Write Your Own Recipe

Directions

1. Choose 3+ items from list below and write them on your ingredients list on the next page.
2. Think about what you want to make.
3. Write down any other ingredients you will need.
4. Draw a picture of the dish and give it a name.
5. Write your recipe directions. Look at the Cooking Terms for some words to include.

Leftover Ingredients: Choose three or more

1 Bagel	Opened Can of Corn	Half Lemon
2 Tomatoes	Lettuce	Handful Grapes
½ Onion	Handful of Spinach	Leftover Meatballs
Cheddar Cheese	2 Small Cooked Potatoes	½ cup Brown Rice
One Boiled Egg		Steamed broccoli

Lesson 4: Write Your Own Recipe

Recipe Name

Ingredients

Picture

Directions

Lesson 4: Cooking Terms

🟥 Use these cooking words to write your recipe

Bake	to cook with medium heat, usually in an oven
Boil	to heat a liquid until the surface bubbles continuously
Broil	to cook under strong and direct heat
Chop	to cut solid food into chunks or medium-sized pieces
Deep Fry	to cook in a deep layer of very hot oil
Dice	to chop into extremely small pieces
Fry	to cook in very hot oil
Garnish	to add a final decorative or flavorful touch on a dish
Grate	to rub food on a grater to make shreds
Grill	to cook over direct heat
Knead	to press dough (i.e., for bread) repeatedly with hands
Marinate	to pre-mix food with wet or dry seasonings; helps develop the flavor as well as moisturize it
Mince	to cut solid food into small cubes of the same size
Puree	to blend until smooth
Roast	to cook in very hot oil
Saute	to cook/brown food in a small amount of hot oil
Simmer	to cook slowly in liquid over low heat, with bubbles barely forming on the surface
Slice	to cut food into strips
Steam	to cook with steam, usually in a closed container
Whip/Whisk	to beat quickly, in order to add air and volume to food

Lesson 4: Recipe

French Toast Sticks

🕐 15 minutes

Ingredients

6 Bread Slices, cut into sticks

2 Eggs

½ cup Milk

½ tsp. Vanilla Extract

½ tsp. Cinnamon

1 Tbsp. Butter

Optional: Powdered Sugar or Maple Syrup

Serves 4

Recipe Directions

1. Whisk egg with milk, vanilla, and cinnamon in medium bowl.
2. Soak bread sticks in egg mixture, one at a time—turn over for even coverage.
3. Melt butter in frying pan and cook sticks for about 2 minutes per side.

Optional cooking method: Set on a baking sheet and bake in the oven at 400 degrees, for 6 minutes.

Chef's Tips

Top with yogurt and berries.

Try topping with sliced bananas and peanut butter.

Stale or dried out bread makes the best french toast.

Try leftover hotdog or hamburger buns, rolls, or even croissants.

Lesson 4: Recipe

Italian Bread Salad

🕒 15 minutes

Ingredients

4 tomatoes, diced

2 cups Stale or Toasted Bread, cubed

4 Tbsp. Olive Oil

1 tsp. Salt

1 Tbsp. Wine Vinegar (red or white)

1 Clove Garlic, minced

Salt and Pepper, to taste

Optional: Chopped basil

Serves 4

Recipe Directions

1. Mix diced tomatoes, 4 Tbsp of olive oil, and ½ tsp. salt and put aside for 5-10 minutes.

2. Place cubed bread in a bowl.

3. Mix 2 Tbsp. olive oil, ½ tsp. salt, wine vinegar, and minced garlic.

4. Add tomato mix and oil/vinegar dressing into bread bowl and add a sprinkle of salt and pepper to taste. Toss and sprinkle with basil.

Chef's Tips

| Try whole wheat, sourdough, or a baguette. | Use fresh oregano, parsley, rosemary, thyme, or mint. |

Lesson 5:
Do I Throw It Out?

Lesson 5: Package Smart

Natural packaging—the skins and peels of produce, can go into compost bins, if you have one. Containers, boxes, and bags can be reused or recycled. Many towns and cities have recycling and composting bins so you can keep these items out of the landfill.

Check off what items go into your city or town's bins from this list.

Landfill
- ☐ single-use packaging that can't be easily reused or recycled (very soft plastics, such as sandwich bags, plastic wrap)
- ☐ styrofoam and other non-recyclable materials
- ☐ packaging that combines materials (plastic- or foil-coated cartons)
- ☐ animal feces and diapers

Recycle
- ☐ yogurt containers
- ☐ to-go packaging
- ☐ aluminum bottles and cans
- ☐ clean glass or plastic containers (a little residue is usually okay)
- ☐ clean paper products, like boxes and paper bags

Compostable
- ☐ grass and leaves from the yard
- ☐ fruit and vegetable scraps
- ☐ meat scraps
- ☐ compostable packaging and bags
- ☐ waxed cardboard

6 Tips for wasting less packaging

Avoid buying food storage containers- save used jars and containers with lids instead.

Some glass and hard plastic packaging can be used for eating from, drinking from, or storing foods.

Buy in bulk using old bags and lidded jars.

Carry reusable bottles and even cutlery for eating on the go.

When shopping, choose items that come with less packaging when possible.

Re-use your paper and plastic bags

Lesson 5: Garden Composting 101

You can turn food scraps and some packaging into compost you can use for plants, at home or in the garden.

1. What belongs in your pile?

Chop larger materials into smaller pieces.
Use slightly more "browns" than "greens"

Browns (carbon)
- Dried plant material
- Paper towels, napkins and plates
- Newspaper
- Wood ash
- Untreated sawdust

Water
- Add water as you build the pile.
- Keep as moist as a wrung-out sponge.

Greens (Nitrogen)
- Grass clippings
- Coffee grounds
- Vegetables
- Herbivore manure
- Fruit
- Grains

What doesn't belongs in your pile

- Diseased plants
- Weeds with seeds
- Dog or cat poop
- Chemicals
- Meat, fish, poultry
- Dairy
- Treated wood
- Fats, oils, grease
- Compostable packaging or bags

2. Compost Critters

These critters are needed to break down the material:

- Pill bug
- Centipede
- Ant
- Fungi
- Mold
- Worms
- Fruit fly
- Slug
- Beetle
- Spider

3. Is it done?

Your compost is done and ready for harvesting if it is:

- Dark chocolatey brown
- Feels crumbly
- Smells like earth
- Fairly small pieces

Separate any remaining large material such as large pieces of wood with a screen or sifter.

4. Use it as

- Soil conditioner
- Top dressing
- Mulch
- Potting mixture

Lesson 5: Recipe

Hummus and Veggie Wraps

🕐 15 minutes

Ingredients

4 Whole Wheat Tortillas, large or burrito size

1 Green Bell Pepper, sliced

1 Tomato, sliced

2 cups chopped Lettuce or sprouts

1 cup Hummus, prepared

Optional: ½ cup sliced olives

Serves 4

Recipe Directions

1. Spread hummus on tortilla.
2. Layer veggies. Sprinkle with optional olives.
3. Roll up and eat!

Chef's Tips

Make your own hummus:
1 can garbanzo beans, rinsed and drained; ⅓ cup Greek yogurt or olive oil; 1 clove garlic, minced; 1 Tbsp. lemon juice; ½ tsp. cumin, and pinch of salt

Puree everything in a blender or food processor. You can also mash the garbanzo beans up with the back of a fork or potato masher before adding everything else.

Lesson 5: Recipe

Easy Peasy Fried Rice

🕐 15 minutes

Ingredients

3 tsp. Vegetable Oil

2 Eggs

¼ Onion, chopped

½ cup chopped cooked Chicken

1 cup cooked Rice

1 cup chopped vegetables

½ cup Peas

1 Tbsp. Soy Sauce

Serves 4

Recipe Directions

1. In a large skillet or wok, heat 1 tsp vegetable oil.
2. Add eggs and scramble in pan. Remove and set aside.
3. Heat remaining oil. Add onion and sauté until soft.
4. Add rice, chicken, vegetables, peas, and stir.
5. Add soy sauce, eggs, and stir.

Chef's Tips

Leftover rice is best for fried rice.

Instead of chicken, use more eggs.

Look for leftover vegetables from the refrigerator (like carrots, corn, celery, cabbage, broccoli, mushrooms, and cauliflower).